PRINCEWILL LAGANG

Love After Loss: Moving Forward Together

First published by PRINCEWILL LAGANG 2023

Copyright © 2023 by Princewill Lagang

All rights reserved. No part of this publication may be reproduced, stored or transmitted in any form or by any means, electronic, mechanical, photocopying, recording, scanning, or otherwise without written permission from the publisher. It is illegal to copy this book, post it to a website, or distribute it by any other means without permission.

Princewill Lagang asserts the moral right to be identified as the author of this work.

First edition

This book was professionally typeset on Reedsy. Find out more at reedsy.com

Contents

1	Introduction	1
2	Understanding Grief and Loss	3
3	Navigating Emotions Together	5
4	Communication Through Grief	7
5	Reconnecting in the Wake of Loss	9
6	Supporting Each Other's Healing	11
7	Navigating Changes and Adjustments	13
8	Balancing Individual Grief and Partnership	15
9	Finding New Purpose and Meaning	17
10	Remembering and Honoring Together	19
11	Moving Forward as a United Team	21
12	Embracing Love and Life Anew	23

1

Introduction

In the vast tapestry of human experience, few emotions hold as much power and complexity as love. It has the ability to shape destinies, mend broken hearts, and inspire remarkable feats. Yet, for all its beauty, love is often intertwined with loss, heartache, and pain. This dichotomy forms the crux of our exploration as we embark on a journey through the intricate landscape of love and relationships in the aftermath of profound loss.

At its core, this narrative seeks to delve into the profound impact of love on individuals who have endured the agony of loss. Grief and heartbreak, whether through the death of a loved one, the dissolution of a partnership, or the separation from a close friend, leave an indelible mark on the human psyche. These experiences alter our perception of the world, casting shadows of doubt and despair. However, it is precisely within the contours of these shadows that the transformative power of love emerges.

As we navigate the chapters that follow, we will encounter individuals who have found themselves at the crossroads of love and loss. Their stories will reveal the intricacies of grief, the tumultuous journey of healing, and the ways in which love can serve as both a balm and a catalyst for growth. Through their narratives, we will explore how forging new connections and nurturing existing relationships can provide a path towards restoration.

The pages ahead will illuminate the ways in which love acts as a potent force of change. It is within the warmth of love's embrace that characters begin to mend their shattered souls. We will witness how shared laughter, heartfelt conversations, and the comfort of a caring touch can begin to bridge the chasm that loss often leaves behind. The storylines will emphasize the significance of vulnerability and the courage it takes to open one's heart once more, despite the fear of being hurt again.

In essence, this narrative underscores that the journey towards healing and growth after loss is intrinsically tied to the exploration of love and relationships. It is not an easy path, for the scars of loss can run deep. However, it is a path worth treading, for it is through love that we discover the resilience of the human spirit and the capacity to find beauty even in the midst of pain.

As we turn the page to embark on this expedition, let us keep in mind that the human experience is marked by a tapestry of emotions, and the threads of love and loss are inextricably woven together. Through the stories of those who have braved this tumultuous terrain, we shall unravel the layers of emotions, experiences, and revelations that define our understanding of love after loss.

2

Understanding Grief and Loss

Grief, that profound and universal emotion, is an experience that touches every life sooner or later. It is a testament to the depth of our connections and the love we hold for those who are no longer with us. In this chapter, we embark on an exploration of the intricate landscape of grief and loss, unraveling its various forms, its impact on individuals and relationships, and the complex emotional journey it entails.

Loss comes in many forms—death, separation, divorce, the end of a friendship, the loss of a job, or even the loss of a sense of self. Each type of loss brings with it a unique set of emotions and challenges. The suddenness of death leaves us in shock and disbelief, grappling with an absence that seems inconceivable. The gradual fading away of a relationship due to distance or time erodes our connections slowly, often leaving a sense of longing and nostalgia in its wake. The termination of a partnership, whether romantic or platonic, can usher in feelings of rejection, abandonment, and heartache.

The impact of loss extends beyond the individual, rippling through the fabric of relationships. Friends and family members may grapple with their own grief while also seeking to provide support to the bereaved.

Misunderstandings and conflicts can arise as people attempt to navigate their own emotions while also being there for others. The dynamic of relationships can shift drastically in the face of loss, sometimes deepening connections and at other times causing them to fracture.

The grieving process is far from linear; it is a complex and often messy journey. It is marked by a range of emotions that may surface unpredictably—denial, anger, bargaining, depression, and acceptance. These emotions are not experienced in any particular order, and individuals may find themselves cycling through them repeatedly. The process is deeply personal, influenced by cultural, social, and personal factors. Some may choose to confront grief head-on, seeking therapy or support groups, while others may attempt to bury their pain, only for it to resurface later.

As we delve into the emotional complexities of grief and loss, it is crucial to recognize that there is no right or wrong way to grieve. Each person's journey is unique, shaped by their experiences, coping mechanisms, and support networks. It is through understanding and empathy that we can create a space for individuals to process their emotions in their own time and in their own way.

In the chapters ahead, we will meet characters who grapple with different types of loss, each navigating the tumultuous sea of grief in their own way. Their stories will illuminate the various facets of the grieving process and shed light on the resilience of the human spirit in the face of heart-wrenching sorrow. Through their narratives, we will gain a deeper appreciation for the complexity of grief and the ways in which it shapes our understanding of love and relationships in the aftermath of loss.

3

Navigating Emotions Together

Loss has an uncanny ability to both unite and test the bonds of love and relationships. In this chapter, we embark on a journey through the complex terrain of emotions that partners experience after facing loss. We delve into the challenges and triumphs of navigating these emotions together, exploring the significance of mutual support, empathy, and understanding.

When loss strikes, partners find themselves grappling with a kaleidoscope of emotions. From sorrow and anger to guilt and confusion, each emotion is a testament to the profound impact that the absence of a loved one can have. These emotions often ebb and flow, sometimes intertwining in ways that are difficult to unravel. Partners may discover that their emotional responses differ, leading to moments of miscommunication and misunderstanding. Yet, it is within this emotional turmoil that the potential for growth and healing resides.

The foundation of a partnership is put to the test during times of loss. The ability to navigate these emotions together is a testament to the strength of the relationship. It is a journey that requires patience, active listening, and a willingness to offer support even when one's own grief is overwhelming. Partners must find ways to create a safe space where both can express their feelings openly, without judgment or expectation.

Mutual support and understanding become vital lifelines in this turbulent journey. Partners who can recognize the validity of each other's emotions and experiences lay the groundwork for a more resilient connection. Through vulnerability and shared empathy, they begin to bridge the gap between their differing emotional landscapes. This support doesn't mean erasing one's own pain; rather, it involves holding space for both individual grief and shared healing.

Communication, during this phase, takes on an even more crucial role. Partners must navigate conversations about grief, loss, and their emotions with sensitivity. The ability to listen without attempting to fix or solve, and to offer a shoulder to lean on without judgment, cultivates a bond that can withstand even the most challenging circumstances. Partners who can express their needs and provide validation for each other's emotions foster an environment of emotional intimacy that serves as a source of strength.

As we journey through the narratives of our characters, we will witness the intricacies of partners navigating emotions together after loss. Their stories will showcase the moments of connection and dissonance, the trials and triumphs, and the gradual weaving of a tapestry of shared understanding. Through their experiences, we learn that while grief may cast shadows, it is the light of mutual support and empathetic companionship that guides partners towards healing and growth.

4

Communication Through Grief

In the landscape of grief, effective communication becomes a compass guiding partners through the tumultuous seas of emotions. In this chapter, we delve into the pivotal role that communication plays in navigating the journey of grief together. We explore techniques for expressing feelings and listening to one another with empathy and compassion, fostering a space where partners can find solace and understanding in each other's presence.

Grief is a deeply personal experience, and the ways in which individuals express their emotions can vary significantly. Partners may find themselves grappling with emotions that are difficult to put into words or may be unsure of how to support each other amidst their own pain. Here, the art of communication becomes essential. It is through effective communication that partners can bridge the gap between their feelings, understand each other's perspectives, and build a foundation of trust.

One of the cornerstones of effective communication during grief is active listening. This involves giving each other undivided attention and truly seeking to understand the emotions being shared. Active listening entails not just hearing the words being spoken, but also picking up on the nuances of tone, body language, and emotions that lie beneath the surface. By validating each other's emotions and providing a safe space to express them, partners can create an environment of emotional intimacy.

Expressing feelings requires vulnerability. Partners must feel comfortable sharing their emotions without fear of judgment or rejection. Honest and open dialogue helps partners understand each other's unique experiences and emotions, enabling them to walk alongside each other on this journey. Techniques such as "I statements" can be incredibly helpful—phrases like "I feel" or "I need" can foster a sense of safety and promote open discussion.

It's important to acknowledge that emotions can be overwhelming, and partners may occasionally find themselves at a loss for words. Nonverbal communication, such as touch, gestures, and facial expressions, can convey emotions just as powerfully. Sometimes, the simple act of being present and offering a comforting hug can speak volumes when words fall short.

Furthermore, the journey of grief may uncover unresolved conflicts or unspoken feelings within a relationship. Partners must be willing to address these issues, using "I statements" and a non-blaming approach to avoid escalating tensions. By doing so, they can create a space for healing not only from the loss itself but also from any lingering emotional wounds.

As we delve into the lives of our characters, we will witness the evolution of their communication strategies as they navigate grief together. Their stories will illustrate the power of listening, validation, and vulnerability in building a bridge of understanding. Through their experiences, we will learn that effective communication is not about having all the answers but about creating a safe haven where partners can share their grief, support each other, and find solace in their shared journey.

5

Reconnecting in the Wake of Loss

L oss has a profound way of reshaping the landscape of a relationship, altering the dynamics between partners. In this chapter, we delve into the intricate process of reconnecting as a couple after experiencing loss. We explore the challenges that may arise and provide strategies for rebuilding intimacy and connection, fostering a renewed sense of togetherness.

After facing loss, couples often find themselves navigating uncharted emotional territory. The grief they experience may lead to a sense of isolation or emotional distance, as partners grapple with their individual pain. However, the journey towards reconnection is marked by the shared desire to rebuild and heal together.

One of the initial steps towards reconnection is acknowledging that both partners are experiencing grief, albeit in their own ways. Partners must validate each other's emotions and recognize that their unique responses are a natural part of the grieving process. The act of empathetic validation paves the way for a deeper understanding of each other's perspectives.

Creating space for open and honest conversations is pivotal in the process of reconnection. Partners should feel comfortable sharing their feelings and experiences, even if they differ from their partner's. By expressing vulnerability and actively listening, couples can bridge the emotional gap that may have developed in the aftermath of loss.

Shared rituals and activities can serve as bridges to reconnecting. Engaging in activities that hold positive memories or embarking on new experiences together can help partners rediscover the joy they once found in each other's company. These shared moments provide an opportunity to focus on the present and foster new connections.

Rebuilding intimacy goes beyond physical touch; it encompasses emotional closeness as well. Partners can practice emotional intimacy by creating a space for each other's feelings, discussing hopes and fears, and sharing moments of vulnerability. This exchange of emotions fosters a sense of connection that can be deeply healing.

As couples navigate the process of reconnection, they must be patient with themselves and with each other. Healing takes time, and progress may not always be linear. It's important to acknowledge setbacks and celebrate even the smallest victories along the way.

Through the stories of our characters, we will witness the various ways in which couples find their way back to each other after loss. Their narratives will highlight the challenges they face, the strategies they employ, and the transformative power of perseverance. These stories serve as a testament to the human spirit's capacity to heal and grow, even in the face of the most heart-wrenching experiences.

6

Supporting Each Other's Healing

In the aftermath of loss, partners often find themselves standing at the crossroads of their grief, searching for ways to navigate the path towards healing. This chapter delves into the crucial role of providing comfort and support to one another during times of grief. We explore the various ways partners can create a safe and nurturing environment that encourages the sharing of emotions and facilitates healing.

Loss carries a heavy emotional burden, and it's in the gentle embrace of a partner's support that healing can begin to take root. Partners who can offer empathy, patience, and understanding create a safe haven where emotions can be expressed openly and without judgment. This support is especially vital during the early stages of grief, when emotions are often raw and intense.

One of the foundational elements of providing support is validating each other's emotions. Partners must recognize that grief is a complex journey, and it's natural for emotions to fluctuate. Creating an atmosphere where both partners can express their feelings, whether they are anger, sadness, guilt, or confusion, helps to alleviate the isolation that grief can bring.

Active listening, as discussed earlier, remains a cornerstone of supporting each other's healing. Partners must be present and fully engaged in conversations, offering their undivided attention and validating the emotions being shared. This process of listening without judgment creates a space where partners feel heard and understood.

Offering physical comfort is equally significant. Sometimes, a reassuring touch, a hug, or simply holding each other's hand can convey emotions that words struggle to express. Physical closeness can serve as a powerful means of connection, reminding partners that they are not alone in their pain.

While providing comfort, it's important to remember that everyone's healing journey is unique. Partners must respect each other's coping mechanisms and refrain from trying to "fix" the other person's pain. Instead, they can ask open-ended questions that encourage conversation, such as "How are you feeling today?" or "Is there anything you'd like to talk about?"

In addition to offering support, partners must also prioritize self-care. Grief can be draining, and taking care of one's own emotional well-being allows for a stronger foundation to support each other. Partners can encourage activities that bring joy, whether that's engaging in hobbies, spending time in nature, or seeking professional help when needed.

Through the stories of our characters, we will witness the ways in which partners extend their support to one another during times of grief. Their narratives will highlight the importance of empathy, patience, and creating a safe space for shared vulnerability. These stories serve as a reminder that while grief may cast shadows, the light of mutual support can guide partners towards a path of healing and renewal.

7

Navigating Changes and Adjustments

Loss has a way of reshaping the very fabric of our lives, bringing with it changes that ripple through every aspect of our existence. In this chapter, we explore how loss can lead to shifts in roles, routines, and dynamics within a relationship. We delve into the challenges partners face as they adapt to these changes and offer guidance on maintaining the foundation of their relationship amid the shifting landscape.

Grief can introduce unexpected changes, both big and small, that impact the dynamics between partners. Roles that were once clearly defined may blur, routines may be disrupted, and familiar interactions may evolve. These shifts can be disorienting, as partners grapple with new responsibilities and altered expectations.

One of the key steps in navigating changes is acknowledging their existence and discussing them openly. Partners must communicate their needs, concerns, and hopes as they navigate the adjustments together. This dialogue creates a shared understanding of the challenges each partner faces, fostering a sense of unity even in the midst of change.

As roles evolve, it's important to recognize that partners may experience differing emotional responses. Some may seek solace in their responsibilities, while others may find certain tasks triggering. This understanding allows for flexibility and provides space for partners to express their feelings without judgment.

Adjusting to changes also requires a willingness to redefine routines. The daily patterns that once brought comfort may now serve as reminders of the loss. Partners can collaborate to create new routines that incorporate self-care, shared activities, and moments of connection. This adaptation fosters an environment of growth and healing.

In the face of these changes, partners must also remember to show compassion towards each other. Grief can manifest in various ways, and there may be moments of frustration or misunderstanding. Providing space for each other's emotions and expressing empathy cultivates a foundation of support that can weather even the most challenging adjustments.

While navigating changes, it's important to maintain the foundation of the relationship. Partners can intentionally set aside time to connect and strengthen their bond. This might involve participating in activities they once enjoyed, exploring new hobbies together, or simply spending quality time engaging in heartfelt conversations.

Through the stories of our characters, we will witness the evolution of their relationships as they navigate changes and adjustments after loss. Their narratives will underscore the importance of flexibility, communication, and empathy in maintaining the connection between partners. These stories serve as a testament to the resilience of love, even in the face of profound shifts, and remind us that adapting to change can lead to growth and renewal.

8

Balancing Individual Grief and Partnership

Grief is an intricate dance between personal pain and shared connection. In this chapter, we delve into the delicate balance between individual grief and maintaining a partnership after loss. We explore the challenges partners face as they strive to be there for each other while also addressing their own needs and emotions.

Grief is a deeply personal journey, and each partner may experience it differently. The challenge lies in recognizing the validity of both individual grief and the collective bond of the partnership. Partners must acknowledge that while they share a profound connection, their experiences of loss are uniquely their own.

Maintaining a relationship in the wake of loss requires empathy and understanding. Partners must honor each other's grief, offering space for individual emotions to unfold without judgment. This process involves listening actively, validating feelings, and expressing compassion for the pain being experienced.

Amidst this, partners may find themselves grappling with a complex set of emotions. The desire to be a source of comfort for each other may clash with the need to confront one's own sorrow. Striking a balance between offering support and allowing oneself to grieve can be a nuanced endeavor.

Open communication is paramount in this process. Partners must discuss their emotional needs, boundaries, and moments when they require space to process their own grief. These conversations create a roadmap for navigating individual healing while preserving the connection that is at the heart of the relationship.

One of the challenges is the potential for misunderstandings or hurt feelings to arise. Partners may unintentionally interpret each other's actions as neglect or indifference when, in reality, they are grappling with their own emotions. Patience and ongoing dialogue are essential in overcoming these obstacles.

It's also crucial for partners to prioritize self-care. Attending to one's emotional well-being ensures that they have the capacity to offer genuine support to their partner. Engaging in activities that bring joy, seeking therapy, or practicing mindfulness are all strategies that can contribute to maintaining emotional balance.

Through the stories of our characters, we will witness the intricate dance of balancing individual grief and partnership. Their narratives will reveal the complexities, moments of understanding, and the challenges they face as they navigate their journeys of healing alongside their partner. These stories underscore that while grief may feel isolating, the strength of connection lies in the shared effort to balance individual healing and collective growth.

9

Finding New Purpose and Meaning

In the wake of loss, the journey to healing often leads couples to a profound crossroads—a juncture where grief can transform into a catalyst for new purpose and meaning. This chapter delves into the ways couples can rediscover purpose amid their grief, finding renewed meaning in their lives and relationship. Through the stories of couples who channeled their pain into positive actions, we explore the transformative power of turning sorrow into purpose.

Loss can shatter our sense of direction and purpose, leaving a void that can feel insurmountable. Yet, within this void lies an opportunity for couples to find new meaning and goals that honor the memory of their loved ones. By recognizing the potential for growth, partners can begin to shift their perspective from the pain of the past to the promise of the future.

One of the avenues for finding new purpose is through acts of kindness and service. Couples can channel their grief into actions that positively impact others, whether through volunteering, supporting a charitable cause, or initiating projects that honor the legacy of their loved ones. These acts not only create a sense of purpose but also offer a way to give back to the community.

Creating new traditions and rituals can also infuse life with a sense of purpose. Partners can embark on shared endeavors that honor their loved one's memory and celebrate their life. These rituals can be as simple as planting a memorial garden, organizing an annual event, or dedicating time to a hobby that was meaningful to the person who is no longer present.

Another pathway to purpose involves personal growth and transformation. Partners can support each other in pursuing new goals, whether it's embarking on a creative endeavor, pursuing education, or exploring new experiences. These endeavors serve as a testament to the resilience of the human spirit and the capacity to find light even in the darkest of times.

The stories of our characters will highlight the myriad ways couples find new purpose and meaning after loss. From founding support groups to advocate for change to embarking on charitable ventures that honor their loved one's memory, their journeys serve as inspiration for others who may be grappling with similar challenges. These stories underscore the capacity for resilience, growth, and the ability to transform grief into a force for positive change and renewed purpose.

10

Remembering and Honoring Together

As time passes, the memories of a loved one lost continue to shape the lives of those left behind. In this final chapter, we delve into the ways couples can remember and honor the person they've lost, creating a legacy that strengthens their bond and offers comfort. By exploring shared remembrance, we witness the profound impact that keeping memories alive can have on the healing journey of partners.

Grief may change with time, but the memories of a loved one remain etched in the heart. Partners can find solace and connection in the act of remembering together. This shared remembrance not only honors the person who has passed but also serves as a testament to the enduring love that binds partners.

Creating rituals of remembrance can help partners keep the memory of their loved one alive. These rituals can be as simple as lighting a candle on significant dates, sharing stories during family gatherings, or visiting a meaningful place. These actions offer a way to incorporate the presence of the loved one into everyday life.

Incorporating the memory of the loved one into shared experiences fosters a sense of continuity. Partners can embark on journeys or activities that hold a special place in their hearts, carrying the spirit of their loved one with them. This form of "living remembrance" becomes a way to keep the connection alive in moments of joy and growth.

Couples can also create tangible memorials that celebrate the life and impact of their loved one. This might involve establishing scholarships, contributing to charitable causes, or dedicating a place or object in their memory. These memorials serve as a source of comfort and a way to channel grief into actions that honor the person's legacy.

Through the stories of our characters, we witness the diverse ways in which couples remember and honor their loved ones. From creating art installations to participating in charitable events, their actions underscore the enduring nature of love and the ways in which shared remembrance strengthens the bond between partners. These stories serve as a reminder that even as grief transforms, the memory of a loved one can continue to inspire and uplift, creating a legacy of love that endures through time.

11

Moving Forward as a United Team

After traversing the landscape of grief and loss, partners often find themselves at a juncture where healing and growth beckon. In this final chapter, we delve into the journey of moving forward as a united team, navigating the path of healing, renewal, and shared purpose. We explore strategies for supporting each other as partners embark on this new chapter of their lives together.

Healing is not a linear journey; it's a process that requires time, patience, and unwavering support. Partners who have weathered the storms of grief together have a unique foundation on which to build their future. As they move forward, they become a united team, drawing strength from their shared experiences.

One of the key strategies for moving forward is fostering open communication. Partners must continue to check in with each other about their emotions, needs, and goals. This ongoing dialogue ensures that both partners remain attuned to each other's feelings and can provide support when it's most needed.

Setting joint goals is another way to solidify the bond between partners. These goals can be related to personal growth, relationship enrichment, or shared endeavors. Having something to work towards together infuses life with purpose and allows partners to continue growing as a united force.

Embracing gratitude is a powerful tool for moving forward. While the pain of loss may always be present, it's important to focus on the positive moments that life continues to offer. Partners can make an intentional effort to acknowledge the joy, love, and beauty that surround them, even in the midst of sorrow.

Seeking professional help when needed is a sign of strength, not weakness. Partners who are navigating complex emotions may benefit from individual or couples therapy. A therapist can offer guidance, tools, and a safe space to explore the nuances of grief and healing.

Finally, it's important to remember that moving forward doesn't mean forgetting the person who was lost. Partners can continue to honor their memory through shared rituals, acts of kindness, and meaningful conversations. The love that was shared remains a constant source of inspiration and connection.

Through the stories of our characters, we will witness the ways in which partners move forward as a united team after loss. Their narratives will reflect the challenges, triumphs, and the enduring love that propels them toward a future imbued with hope. These stories serve as a testament to the strength of human resilience and the power of love to guide couples through even the darkest of times.

12

Embracing Love and Life Anew

In the tapestry of human experience, the journey of love and loss is one marked by transformation, resilience, and growth. As we reach the final chapter, we reflect on the experience of finding love after loss and the profound lessons that have emerged from this exploration. This chapter summarizes the key takeaways and offers guidance for embracing a new chapter—a chapter that is shaped by the courage to love and live anew.

Love has an incredible capacity to mend and renew. While the pain of loss may linger, the human heart is remarkably resilient, capable of finding love once again. Partners who have navigated the depths of grief together may find that the bond forged through shared sorrow becomes a foundation on which to build a future of love and connection.

One of the key takeaways is the importance of honoring one's own grief and that of their partner. The journey of healing is multifaceted, and giving space for individual emotions while offering unwavering support cultivates an environment of mutual understanding and empathy.

Effective communication remains the cornerstone of any relationship, especially one that has experienced loss. Partners must continue to actively listen, express their feelings, and adapt their communication as they embrace this new chapter together. This ongoing dialogue creates a safe space where emotions can be shared openly and honestly.

Embracing a new chapter involves looking forward with hope while honoring the past. The memories of the loved one who was lost remain an integral part of the couple's narrative. Partners can continue to celebrate their legacy through shared rituals, conversations, and acts of kindness.

As partners embark on this new chapter, they must be patient with themselves and with each other. Healing is a nonlinear process, and setbacks are a natural part of the journey. Partners should celebrate their progress and remember that growth often arises from moments of challenge.

Ultimately, embracing love and life anew is an act of courage. It's a testament to the human spirit's capacity to heal, to love, and to find meaning even in the face of profound loss. As partners step into this new chapter, they carry with them the lessons learned, the memories cherished, and the boundless potential of a future filled with love, growth, and connection.

Through the stories of our characters, we have witnessed the complexities of love and loss, the challenges and triumphs, and the enduring power of human resilience. As we close this chapter, let us remember that the journey of healing is ongoing, and the capacity to embrace love and life anew is a reflection of the remarkable strength within us all.

Conclusion: Love's Transformative Journey After Loss

In the tapestry of our lives, the threads of love and loss are inextricably woven together. As we conclude this exploration of love's journey after loss, we are reminded that within the depths of sorrow lies the potential for healing, growth, and renewal. The stories we've encountered have illuminated the complexities of navigating grief as a united team, finding solace in shared experiences, and embracing new chapters that honor the past while embracing the future.

Throughout this narrative, one resounding truth has emerged: love is an incomparable force of healing and growth. It is within the embrace of a partner's support that wounds begin to mend and the human spirit rekindles its light. Love has the power to transform grief into purpose, to forge connections that can withstand even the most profound challenges, and to offer a beacon of hope in the face of heartache.

The journey of love after loss is not without its struggles, but it is a journey that is marked by profound empathy, patience, and openness. Partners must extend grace to each other as they navigate the labyrinth of emotions, embracing the understanding that healing takes time and the path is not always linear.

Empathy remains a guiding star throughout this journey. The ability to truly listen, to validate each other's emotions, and to stand shoulder to shoulder through moments of pain and joy is a testament to the strength of the human spirit. Patience, too, is an invaluable companion. Just as grief ebbs and flows, so does the process of healing. Partners must honor their individual paces, offering unwavering support even in moments of darkness.

The journey of love after loss is a profound testament to the indomitable human spirit's capacity to endure, to find solace in shared connection, and to discover beauty amid pain. As we reflect on the stories of our characters and the wisdom gained from their experiences, we are invited to embrace this journey with open hearts, knowing that love is a powerful source of healing, growth, and transformation. May we all navigate this path with empathy, patience, and a profound belief in the enduring power of love.

www.ingramcontent.com/pod-product-compliance
Lightning Source LLC
LaVergne TN
LVHW020743090526
838202LV00057BA/6211